BRISTOL TRACTION

Hugh Llewelyn

AMBERLEY

First published 2019

Amberley Publishing
The Hill, Stroud
Gloucestershire, GL5 4EP

www.amberley-books.com

Copyright © Hugh Llewelyn, 2019

The right of Hugh Llewelyn to be identified as
the Author of this work has been asserted in
accordance with the Copyrights, Designs and
Patents Act 1988.

ISBN 978 1 4456 7805 4 (print)
ISBN 978 1 4456 7806 1 (ebook)

British Library Cataloguing in Publication Data.
A catalogue record for this book is available from
the British Library.

Origination by Amberley Publishing.
Printed in the UK.

Contents

Introduction

This book is not a comprehensive record of modern traction in the Bristol area; rather, it is simply a selection of photographs that I have taken from the early 1960s to the present day. Brought up in South Wales, I occasionally visited Bristol in the 1960s for such events as open days at Bristol Bath Road TMD. My first jobs were in Sussex and London but in the mid-1970s my career took me to Bristol. I lived in Backwell, on the line to Weston-super-Mare, for many years before moving to Bristol itself (Stapleton – not too far from Stapleton Road station). Since retirement, I have moved to Keynsham on the main line to Bath. Although the Bristol area did not have the huge range of traction that London had, nonetheless variety there was aplenty in the 1970s and 1980s. That variety has diminished considerably since privatisation in the mid-1990s, such that passenger operations are dominated by the Great Western Railway with just a leavening of Cross Country and South Western Railway services. Freight, especially coal traffic, which was once so plentiful, is just a shadow of its former self and dominated by the 'Sheds' of DB Cargo and Freightliner. Despite that, it is still fair to say that there is a lot to hold the interest of the railway enthusiast in Bristol and its hinterland. I have taken a very liberal view of what constitutes the city environs and have included areas that once fell into the entirely logical (but deeply unpopular locally) county of Avon.

The photographs are simply a personal record of modern traction ranging from 'heritage' DMUs and 'classic' diesel locomotives to present-day HSTs, Hitachi IEPs and post-privatisation American-designed freight locos. The sheer ubiquity of HSTs since the late 1970s inevitably results in that class having been photographed by me more often than anything else. It is fortunate that the HST is such an iconic design. It is a shame that after so many years of sterling service, they are finally being displaced by the IEPs.

Most photographs are of trains in normal service but a few preserved locomotives hauling specials are included, plus a few on the Avon Valley Railway, a heritage line just a short distance from where I live. The AVR has done much to preserve the 'feel' of a branch line (although it was once a main cross-country line!) in BR days. Further, I have been fairly descriptive about the liveries worn since this is a particular interest of mine.

Despite the personal bias of this book, I believe that the changing nature of both the traction and the locations over the decades should provide enough interest and enjoyment for everyone.

I have arranged the chapters on the basis of classes rather than geographical location, which allows the changing liveries of the more common classes to be compared.

Chapter 1

Shunters (Classes 07 and 08)

Preserved Ruston & Hornsby Class 07 275 hp 0-6-0 No. 07 010 (ex-No. D2944) in BR Rail Blue livery is seen at Bitton on the Avon Valley Railway, 19 October 2014. The 07s were built specially for use in Southampton Docks, where a powerful shunter able to negotiate tight curves was needed. They took over from the USA 0-6-0Ts.

DB Schenker BR/English Electric Class 08 350 hp 0-6-0 shunter No. 08 663 *St Silas* (originally No. D3830) in the heritage livery of BR Rail Blue is pictured at the St Philip's Marsh HST 40th Anniversary Open Day, 2 May 2016.

Another BR/English Electric Class 08 shunter painted in a heritage livery appeared at the St Philip's Marsh HST 40th Anniversary Open Day on 2 May 2016. This was First Great Western's No. 08 822 *Dave Mills* (ex-No. D3990) in BR InterCity Swallow livery. It was acting as the depot shunter.

Chapter 2

English Electric Type 1 (Class 20) and BR Type 2 (Class 25)

The English Electric Type 1 1,000 hp Bo-Bo – later Class 20 under TOPS – is one of the most successful British diesel designs. Seen at Bristol Temple Meads on 11 January 2008 are Class 20/9s Nos 20 905 (previously No. 20 225; originally No. D8325) and No. 20 901 (ex-Nos 20 101 and D8101). They were converted from Class 20/0s for Hunslet-Barclay, subsequently taken over by Direct Rail Services (DRS) and then bought by the Harry Needle Railroad Company. They are freshly repainted in BR Trainload Freight two-tone grey – or should it be three-tone with roofs in a different shade of grey?

A very grimy BR/Beyer Peacock Type 2 (TOPS Class 25/1) 1,250 hp Bo-Bo No. 25 039 (ex-No. D5189) in BR Rail Blue at Bristol Temple Meads heads a Taunton–Cardiff (General) service, October 1975. The first batches of the Class 25s typified BR's lack of concern over the aesthetics of the early diesel designs with a plethora of grilles on the body sides and what proved unnecessary gangways on the cab fronts. The later batches were cleaned up considerably by the Design Research Unit.

Chapter 3

Brush Type 2 (Class 31)

The A1A-A1A Brush Type 2s (later, under TOPS, Class 30 then 31) were criticised at the time of their introduction for having an unpowered axle in each bogie, which was seen as unnecessary deadweight. Nonetheless, once the Class 30's original troublesome Mirrlees engines were replaced by more reliable English Electric ones, the reclassified 31s were one of the most successful and long-lived of BR's early diesel designs. Pictured is one of Wessex Trains' summer Saturdays Bristol Temple Meads–Weymouth services, which at the time were usually formed of a 1,450 hp Brush Class 31/4 hauling air-conditioned Mk 2 coaches. No. 31 452 *Minotaur* (ex-Nos 31 552; 31 452; 31 279; D5809) of Fragonset Railways was on hire to Wessex Trains for this duty on 15 July 2004.

Brush Class 31/1 No. 31 106 *Spalding Town* (ex-No. D5524; previously named *The Blackcountryman*) of Howard Johnston Engineering, but still in the rather drab black livery of defunct Fragonset Railways, is at Bristol Temple Meads on a Network Rail test train, 13 March 2009. Behind is the derelict Royal Mail building, a 'beauty spot' that has greeted people arriving by train into Bristol for many years.

Stabled at Bristol Temple Meads on a Network Rail test train on 1 April 2009 is a work-stained Brush Class 31/4 No. 31 454 (ex-Nos 31 554; 31 454; 31 228; D5654) of RMS Locotec in BR InterCity Swallow livery. It was previously named *The Heart of Wessex*.

Preserved Brush Class 31/1 No. 5580 (also No. 31 162) in Rail Blue was exhibited at the St Philip's Marsh HST 40th Anniversary Open Day on 2 May 2016.

Chapter 4

BRC&W Co. Type 3 (Class 33)

The Birmingham Railway Carriage & Wagon Co. Type 3 (TOPS Class 33) 'Crompton' Bo-Bo was specially produced for BR's Southern Region, which wanted a Type 3 locomotive even though the British Transport Commission did not envisage any need for such a locomotive. Trundling through the carriage washing plant at Bedminster carriage sidings in September 1985 is 1,550 hp Class 33/0 No. 33 023 (ex-No. D6541) in Rail Blue. In the background are the terraces of the aptly named Totterdown.

Fragonset Railways' locomotives were frequently seen at Bristol Temple Meads before that company went under. Seen here on 24 July 2007 is BRC&W Co. Class 33/2 'Crompton' No. 33 202 (ex-No. D6587), which had once carried a variety of names: *Meteor*, *The Burma Star*, and *Dennis G. Robinson*. This particular locomotive had a narrow body to work the tight clearances of the Hastings line.

Chapter 5

English Electric Type 3 (Class 37)

Another great success of British Railways' first generation of diesel designs is the English Electric Type 3 (TOPS Class 37) 1,750 hp Co-Co, despite the BTC not originally commissioning any designs for the Type 3 category. Class 37/0 No. 37 162 (ex-No. D6862) in BR Railfreight Grey creeps through Bristol Temple Meads with a fuel train for Bristol St Philip's Marsh TMD in April 1992.

On a very damp day in June 1994, English Electric Class 37/0 No. 37 407 *Loch Long* (ex-No. 37 305; D6605) in BR Mainline livery is at Bristol Temple Meads with a rake of Mk 1 coaches on a Weymouth service. This loco was later named *Blackpool Tower*.

Looking rather decrepit at Temple Meads on 11 February 2011, English Electric Class 37/0 No. 37 704 (ex-Nos 37 034; D6734) had just been withdrawn by EWS and was in their original livery with 'EW&S' branding rather than the later 'EWS'. Despite its sorry state, it was on its way to a new owner, the Harry Needle Railroad Co. of Barrow Hill, for refurbishment.

Under Temple Meads' impressive roof, Class 37/4 No. 37 423 (ex-Nos 37 296; D6996) of DRS in their Compass livery waits for a green with the Network Rail Project Saloon *Caroline*, 1 July 2008. This locomotive had originally been named *Sir Murray Morrison 1873–1948* and was subsequently renamed *Spirit of the Lakes*. *Caroline* was originally a buffet car of a BR (Eastleigh) Class 202 or '6L' Hastings Line six-car InterCity DEMU converted at Stewarts Lane to the Southern Region General Manager's Saloon and then converted by FM Rail in 2004–5 to the Project Saloon.

Blasting away from Bristol Temple Meads after a signal check are Class 37/6s No. 37 612 (ex-Nos 37 691; 37 179; D6879) and No 37 605 (ex-Nos 37 507; 37 036; D6736, formerly named *Hartlepool Pipe Mill*) of DRS in their early livery on a Bridgwater–Sellafield nuclear flask train, 11 June 2009.

English Electric Class 37/6 No. 37 685 (ex-Nos 37 234; D6934), later named *Loch Arkaig*, and No. 37 676 *Loch Rannoch* (ex-Nos 37 126; D6826) of West Coast Railway Co. approach Abbey Wood on the Weston-super-Mare–Manchester Victoria 'Holy Oakes', 26 March 2011.

On display at the St Philip's Marsh HST 40th Anniversary Open Day on 2 May 2016 was an impressively liveried English Electric Class 37/7 No. 37 884 (formerly Nos 37 183; D6883; once named *Gartcosh*) of Europhoenix with Rail Operations Group branding.

Chapter 6

BR Type 3 and 4 Hydraulics (Classes 35, 42 and 52)

While BR chose to standardise on electric transmission for its diesel locomotives, the Western Region – who, it is said, regarded themselves as the Great Western Region! – somehow managed to go their own way in typical Great Western fashion and chose hydraulic transmission. Probably the best of all the hydraulic designs was the Beyer Peacock Type 3 (TOPS Class 35) 'Hymek' 1,700 hp Bo-Bo. Beautifully restored No. D7017 in BR green with a yellow lower-body stripe and small yellow warning panels was on display at the St Philip's Marsh HST 40th Anniversary Open Day on 2 May 2016. I think this livery suited the 'Hymeks' best – far more pleasing than the later plain Rail Blue. Interestingly, its Maybach engine was originally rated at 1,900 hp but derated to 1,700 hp for BR service. Aesthetically, the 'Hymeks' represented a welcome change from the many bland, even ugly, designs BR had previously procured. The body was designed by Wilkes & Ashmore; their two-window windscreen (the first on BR) and their sloped nose were a precursor of future designs such as the Classes 47, 50, 53 and 56. On the other hand, the raked-forward side-window recess was not perpetuated.

Although not the best quality, this photograph is interesting in that it shows the first of the Pilot Batch of BR (Swindon) Type 4 (TOPS Class 42) 'Warship' Class 2,000 hp B-Bs. No. D800 *Sir Brian Robertson* is on display at an open day at Bristol (Bath Road) depot in October 1965. It is in BR white-lined green livery with small yellow warning panels. The 'Warships' were based on the West German Class V200 locomotives and had an excellent power-to-weight ratio, especially compared to the contemporary heavyweight Class 40 and 'Peak' 1Co-Co1 designs. However, the WR's attempt to go its own separate way to the rest of BR in choosing hydraulic rather than electric transmission for its diesel classes did not succeed in the long run and eventually BR imposed the early withdrawal of the hydraulics as non-standard. But it must be said that the less than impressive reliability record of at least some of the hydraulic designs did not help their case.

Preserved but main line-registered BR (Swindon) Type 4 (TOPS Class 52) 'Western' 2,700 hp C-C No. D1015 *Western Champion* running as classmate No. D1005 *Western Adventurer* pulls away from Temple Meads in a typical cloud of Maybach smoke on the Bristol–Kingswear 'Dartmouth Arrow', 30 August 2008. *Western Adventurer* is in BR maroon livery, generally adopted for coaches but which, perversely, the Western Region also adopted for its locomotives. The two Maybach engines could produce 3,000 hp but were derated for BR service. It is interesting that, because of the very high tractive effort the 'Westerns' produced, Foster Yeoman wanted to buy several to work their Mendip Quarry stone trains when the hydraulics were being withdrawn by BR as 'non-standard'. However, privatised locomotives running on a nationalised railway was too radical a concept to be acceptable at that time. Such an innovation had to await the arrival of the General Motors Class 59s twenty years later.

Chapter 7

English Electric Type 4s
(Classes 40 and 50)

Another preserved locomotive on display at the St Philip's Marsh HST 40th Anniversary Open Day on 2 May 2016 was preserved English Electric Type 4 (TOPS Class 40) 2,000 hp Co-Co No. D213 (later No. 40 013) *Andania* in BR green livery. Although criticised even on their introduction as being an overly conservative design, that very conservativism resulted in the Class 40s being amongst BR's most reliable locomotives.

When a powerful diesel design was needed for the unelectrified portion of the WCML from Preston to Glasgow, the derated Class 47s were deemed inadequate, so a new Type 4 was required. Ironically, English Electric's DP2 prototype, which had lost out to the Class 47 for BR's new standard Type 4, was resurrected but BR wanted something more state of the art. The result was a rebodied and considerably more advanced version of DP2, the Class 50. Initially the Class 50s were all BR had hoped they would be and proved high performers. However, when the WCML electrification was completed to Glasgow, the Class 50s were transferred to the WR, by which time they had been run into the ground. The inevitable result was that the reliability of these highly complex locomotives suffered and their availability plummeted. An extensive refurbishment programme which entailed the removal of some of the most complex features improved matters, although perhaps not as much as had been hoped. Seen approaching Temple Meads on a Paddington–Plymouth service in January 1981 is English Electric Class 50 No. 50 033 *Glorious* (ex-No. D433) in BR Rail Blue livery. It is hauling a rake of air-conditioned Mk 2 coaches plus one Mk 1 restaurant car. No Mk 2 restaurant/buffet/kitchen cars were built as most Mk 1 refreshment cars had been somewhat underused and had plenty of life left in them.

Awaiting departure at Temple Meads on a Plymouth–Birmingham New Street service in January 1981 is work-stained Class 50 No. 50 008 *Thunderer* (ex-No. D408) in BR Rail Blue.

Nearing Temple Meads on a Paddington–Plymouth service in October 1983 is Class 50 No. 50 016 *Barham* (ex-No. D416) in BR Large Logo Blue livery. Note the Mk 1 BG full-brake behind.

Another Class 50 at Bristol (Bath Road) MPD: No. 50 036 (ex-No. D436) *Victorious* in BR Large Logo Rail Blue livery with wrap-around yellow front ends is pictured in May 1989.

A very grimy English Electric Class 50 No. 50 019 (ex-No. D419) *Ramillies* in the early version of the BR Network SouthEast livery approaching Bristol Temple Meads with a parcels train, May 1989. I always thought the Network South East livery, especially the early version, suited the Class 50s well – when clean!

Bristol (Bath Road) TMD always seemed to be packed with interesting locomotives and here we see English Electric Class 50 No. 50 016 (ex-No. D416) *Barham* in the 'Large Logo' variety of BR Rail Blue livery, which also included wrap-around yellow cabs, May 1989.

In well-worn BR Network SouthEast livery is English Electric Class 50 No. 50 032 (ex-No. D432) *Courageous* at Bristol (Bath Road) MPD, May 1989. This broadside perspective gives a good view of the NSE livery.

Although the reliability of the Class 50s when in BR service was often poor, the generous care and attention that the surviving main line-registered examples have had lavished upon them in preservation has resulted in some very fine runs on various main lines. Here, seen departing Temple Meads with sister No. 50 049 *Defiance*, is preserved No. D444 *Exeter* (later No. 50 044) looking very attractive in BR two-tone green livery, incongruously, on the 'Rail Blue Charter' from Manchester to Minehead, 18 October 2008.

Preserved English Electric Class 50 No. 50 035 (ex-No. D435) *Ark Royal* in BR Rail Blue livery at the St Philip's Marsh HST 40th Anniversary Open Day, 2 May 2016. Other Class 50s at the open day were No. 50 007 *Hercules* and No. 50 050 *Fearless*, also in Rail Blue.

Chapter 8

BR Type 4 (Classes 45 and 46)

An unidentified BR (Derby) Class 45/1 1Co-Co1 with divided central headcode panels in BR Rail Blue livery and all yellow front ends passes the now demolished Filton Junction station on a cross-country service in June 1977. The 'Peak' Class 44/45/46s and the English Electric Class 40s were BR's first attempts at a diesel-electric Type 4 and both were very conservative designs, unnecessarily heavy because of their 1Co-Co1 wheel arrangement resulting from BR's desire to have a low axle weight to protect the track. Nonetheless, the 'Peaks' and the Class 40s proved reliable and long-lived.

Here Class 45/0 2,500 hp 1Co-Co1 No. 45 015 (ex-No. D14) draws into Bristol (Temple Meads) on a North East–South West service, January 1981. No. D14 was built with headcode panels but by this time they had been removed.

Storming through Chelvey, near Nailsea & Backwell station, Rail Blue Class 46 No. 46 026 (ex-No. D163) *Leicestershire & Derbyshire Yeomanry* with central headcode panels is on a Cross Country service in August 1978.

Class 46 No. 46 042 approaches the now long-gone Filton Junction station on a Cross Country service in June 1977.

Passing Chelvey is Class 46 No. 46 010 (ex-No. D147) heading for Nailsea & Backwell on a Cross Country service, August 1978.

Again passing Chelvey at speed is Class 46 No. 46 038 (ex-No. D175) with headcodes removed on a Cross Country service, August 1982.

The great length of the BR Type 4 'Peak' class always impressed me. Preserved Class 46 No. D182 was on display at the St Philip's Marsh HST 40th Anniversary Open Day, 2 May 2016. When in BR service No. D182 was subsequently renumbered, firstly No. 46 045 and then, in Departmental use, No. 97 404. It has been restored with central headcode panels and is painted in BR Rail Blue with small yellow warning panels.

Chapter 9

Brush Type 4 (Class 47)

The Brush Type 4s were BR's 'standard' Type 4, which took over from the heavy and somewhat underpowered English Electric Class 40s and BR Class 44/45/46 'Peaks'. However, boosting the 2,300/2,500 hp Sulzer engines of the 'Peaks' to 2,750 hp for the Class 47 Co-Cos proved overambitious and the impressive performance of the Class 47s was at the expense of poor reliability and costly repairs. As a result, the Class 47's Sulzer engines were derated to 2,580 hp, which improved reliability but at the expense of the sparkling performance they had been renowned for. Nevertheless, the derated Class 47s proved very successful and long-lived, examples still being in service today. With Nailsea & Backwell station in the distance, Brush Class 47/4 No. 47 471 (ex-No. D1598) in Rail Blue livery accelerates away with a Cross Country service in August 1982.

Approaching Yatton on a Cross Country service in October 1982 is Brush Class 47/4 No. 47 509 (ex-No. D1953) *Albion* in Rail Blue livery.

With a rake of empty stock behind her, Brush Class 47/4 No. 47 625 (ex-Nos 47 076 and No. D1660; later No. 47 749) *City of Truro* (later named *Resplendent*; *Atlantic College*; *Demelza*) arrives at Bedminster Carriage Sidings, September 1985.

In BR's rather plain Rail Blue livery, Brush Class 47/4 No. 47 558 (ex-Nos 47 027 and D1599; later No. 47 722) *Mayflower* (later *The Queen Mother*) approaches Parson Street on a Cross Country service, July 1985.

What was sometimes confused with InterCity livery was BR's Mainline livery, which differed from the InterCity Swallow livery in having no branding, a lower yellow warning panel which wrapped around the cab and a cab roof which was also yellow. Locomotives in such liveries were intended to be used on passenger duties of lower status than InterCity. Pictured at a time when the 'iconic' Royal Mail building behind Temple Meads was still in operation, Mainline-liveried Brush Class 47/4 No. 47 490 (ex-No. D1725; later No. 47 768) *Bristol Bath Road* (later *Resonant*) is awaiting its next turn of duty in May 1989.

Brush Class 47/0 No. 47 060 *Halewood Silver Jubilee 1988* (ex-No. D1644; later No. 57 008 *Freightliner Explorer, Telford International Railfreight Park June 2009*) in BR Railfreight Distribution grey livery is seen at Bristol (Bath Road) TMD in May 1989.

A rather grimy Brush Class 47/4 No. 47 508 (ex-No. D1952) *SS Great Britain* (ex-*Great Britain*) is in a variety of BR's Mainline livery, which has an all-yellow front end but not a yellow cab roof. It is resting at Bristol (Bath Road) TMD, May 1989.

Trundling into Temple Meads on a Cross Country service in May 1989 is Brush Class 47/4 No. 47 459 (ex-No. D1579) in BR Large Logo Rail Blue livery and wrap-around yellow front end.

In my opinion InterCity Swallow was the best looking of all British Rail's liveries. Here Brush Class 47/4 No. 47 842 (ex-Nos 47 606; 47 081; No. D1666; later No. 47 606; 47 778; formerly named *Irresistible* and originally *Odin*; later named *Duke of Edinburgh's Award*) is at Bristol (Bath Road) TMD, May 1992. Note that the InterCity Swallow livery on the Class 47s had a yellow front end only on the lower cab front immediately below the windscreen.

Two Brush Class 47/7s of BR Rail Express Systems enter Temple Meads on a parcels train in June 1992. No. 47 594 *Resourceful* (ex-Nos 47 035; D1615; later No. 47 739 *Robin of Templecombe*) leads an unidentified sister in RES livery. Unusually, No. 47 594 does not have the RES logo of light blue blocks on a downward extension of the upper body dark grey strip as other RES locomotives did.

Repainted in BR two-tone green livery, Brush Class 47/4 No. 47 833 *Captain Peter Mainsty RN* (ex-Nos 47 608; 47 262; D1962; and later No. 47 778) rests at Bristol (Bath Road) TMD, April 1994. The shades of green look rather odd and I suspect are not truly authentic.

BR's Rail Express Systems' livery was quite an imaginative livery, to my mind. RES's Brush Class 47/7 No. 47 500 (ex-Nos D1943; later No. 47 770 and then No. 47 500 again; formerly named *Great Western*; later renamed *Reserved*) is seen at Bristol (Bath Road) TMD in April 1994.

The Anglia livery indicates that Brush Class 47/7 No. 47 714 (ex-Nos 47 511; D1955, formerly named *Grampian Region*; *Thames*) is a long way from home at Bristol Temple Meads, 24 July 2007. The locomotive had recently been bought by Cotswold Rail for refurbishment. Unfortunately, Cotswold Rail had a short life.

Another purchase by Cotswold Rail was Class 47/4 No. 47 818 *Emily* (ex-Nos 47 663; 47 240; D1917; once named *Strathclyde*). It is in debranded ONE livery at Bristol Temple Meads, 19 May 2008, en route to be refurbished.

Stabled at Stoke Gifford Yard on 4 July 2008 is Colas Rail's Brush Class 47/7 No. 47 727 *Rebecca* (ex-Nos 47 569; 47 047; D1629). It had been named previously *Castell Caerffily/Caerphilly Castle*; *Duke of Edinburgh's Award*; *The Gloucestershire Regiment*.

Pulling out of Temple Meads are preserved but main line-registered Brush Class 47/7 No. D1755 (also numbered at various times Nos 47 161; 47 541; 47 773 and previously named *The Queen Mother* and *Reservist*) in BR two-tone green livery and BRC&W Co. Class 33/0 No. 33 025 *Glen Falloch* (ex-No. D6543; previously named *Sultan* and later named *Seafire*) of the West Coast Railway Co. in their maroon livery. They are hauling the Tyseley–Kingswear 'Port of Dartmouth Royal Regatta Special' on 30 September 2008.

Stabled at Temple Meads on 18 October 2008 is Brush Class 47/4 No. 47 828 *Joe Strummer* (ex-Nos 47 629; 47 266; D1966, previously named *Severn Valley Railway*) of Cotswold Rail in their light grey livery.

Pictured is Class 47/7 No. 47 843 *Vulcan* (ex-Nos 47 623; 47 090; D1676) of Riviera Trains in their unbranded blue livery pausing at Temple Meads on the Nantwich–Penzance 'Devon & Cornwall Explorer' excursion, 1 August 2009.

Cruising towards Filton Abbey Wood are Brush Class 47/4s No. 47 501 *Craftsman* (ex-No. D1944) and No. 47 802 *Pride of Cumbria* (ex-Nos 47 552; 47 259; D1950) of DRS in their 'Compass' livery on the Barrow Hill–Paignton 'Seaside Express' excursion, 15 August 2009.

Brush Class 47/7 No. 47 760 (ex-Nos 47 562; 47 672; 47 562; 47 036; D1617; formerly named *Ribblehead Viaduct*; *Restless*; *Sir William Burrell*) of the West Coast Railway Company entering Temple Meads on the Norwich–Bristol Temple Meads–Cardiff Central 'Cheddar Gorge & Welsh Capital' excursion, 22 August 2009. Note the miniature snow ploughs fitted.

Under the magnificent train shed of Temple Meads is the West Coast Railway Company's Brush Class 47/7 No. 47 786 *Roy Castle MBE* (ex-Nos 47 821; 47 607; 47 138; D1730 and previously named *Royal Worcester*) on the Norwich–Bristol Temple Meads–Cardiff Central 'Cheddar Gorge & Welsh Capital' excursion, 22 August 2009. The design of the train shed has been attributed either to Sir Mathew Digby Wyatt (Brunel's colleague) or Francis Fox (engineer of the Bristol & Exeter Railway) but was probably the latter.

Topping Pilning Bank on a 'Northern Belle' Pullman ECS working from Pengam Sidings, Cardiff, to Bristol on 27 April 2012 is Brush Class 47/7 No. 47 790 (ex-Nos 47 673; 47 593; 47 272; D1973 and previously named *Galloway Princess*; *Dewi Sant/Saint David*; *York Inter City Control*; *Galloway Princess*) of the West Coast Railway Co. in their then new special 'Northern Belle' livery.

Preserved but main line-registered Brush Class 47/7 No. 47 773 (ex-Nos 47 541; 47 161; D1755, formerly named *The Queen Mother*, *Reservist*) in BR two-tone green on a very murky morning speeding through Filton Abbey Wood on the Tyseley–Bristol Temple Meads leg of 'The Cornishman', 28 April 2012.

Brush Class 47/7 No. 47 749 *City of Truro* (ex-Nos 47 625; 47 076; D1660, formerly named *Demelza*; *Atlantic College II*; *Resplendent*; *City of Truro*) of Colas Rail at St Philip's Marsh HST 40th Anniversary Open Day, 2 May 2016.

Chapter 10

Brush Type 4 (Class 57)

With the Class 47s ageing, various operators decided to refurbish them with new General Motors (EMD) engines and other equipment, initially for freight use. The rebuilds were classified 57. One operator that came and went in a short time was Advenza Freight. They chose a rather uninspiring plain blue livery, as seen on Brush Class 57/0 2,580 hp Co-Co No. 57 006 (ex-Nos 47 187; D1837; formerly named *Freightliner Reliance*) stabled at Temple Meads, 11 September 2008.

Arriving at Bristol Temple Meads on a Taunton–Cardiff service on 27 January 2010 is Brush Class 57/3 No. 57 316 (ex-No. 47 290; D1992; previously named *Fab 1*) of Arriva Trains Wales in unbranded plain blue livery on hire to First Great Western at a time when there were insufficient Class 158 DMUs available for the Cardiff Central– Taunton service. The Class 57/3s were the first 'production' conversions of Class 47s for passenger use.

Drawing into Temple Meads is Brush Class 57/3 No. 57 312 *The Hood* (ex-No. 47 330; 47 390; 47 330; D1811; formerly *Tren Nwyddau Amlwwch/Amlwch Freighter* later named *Peter Henderson*; *Solway Princess*) of Virgin Trains on hire to FGW on a Taunton–Cardiff Central service, with a sister Class 57 at the rear, 27 January 2010. The coaches are air-conditioned Mk 2s in InterCity Executive livery.

Top and tailed by Class 57s, a Taunton–Cardiff Central service leaves Temple Meads with, at the rear, No. 57 315 (ex-Nos 47 234; D1911, formerly *The Mole*) of Arriva Trains Wales in their 'Executive' two-tone blue livery on hire to FGW, 27 January 2010. Note most of the Mk 2 coaches are in debranded Anglia livery except for one in BR InterCity Executive livery.

An unidentified Brush Class 57/3 of the West Coast Railway Co. speeds through Keynsham on the Bristol Temple Meads–Rugby 'Cathedrals Express' on 3 September 2015.

Looking resplendent in GWR's retro Brunswick Green livery, Brush Class 57/6 No. 57 603 (ex-No. 47 349; D1830; formerly named *Tintagel Castle*) is on display at the St Philip's Marsh HST 40th Anniversary Open Day, 2 May 2016. Note the number plate behind the cab door window.

Chapter 11

Brush Type 5 (Class 56)

Designed to meet a perceived urgent need for a locomotive to haul an expected increase in coal traffic, the Brush Class 56 Co-Cos were an update of the Class 47s with more powerful 3,250 hp Ruston & Hornsby engines. However, in the event, that increase never materialised, so although the Class 56s were used on coal haulage, they were also used on intermodal and other freight traffic. Bedecked in the rather unimaginative BR Rail Blue livery, Class 56 No. 56 046 waits its next turn of duty at Bristol (Bath Road) TMD in September 1985.

Brush Class 56 No. 56 053 *Sir Morgannwg Ganol/County of Mid Glamorgan* in BR Railfreight Construction livery and yellow lower cab front is seen at Bristol (Bath Road) TMD, May 1989.

On display at the St Philip's Marsh HST 40th Anniversary Open Day, 2 May 2016, is Brush Class 56 No. 56 098 *Lost Boys 68-88* of UK Rail Leasing Ltd in retro BR Large Logo Railfreight Grey livery.

Chapter 12

Brush Type 5 (Class 60)

The last diesel locomotives of British design and British build are the Brush 3,100 hp Class 60 Co-Cos. Crawling through Westerleigh village, heading for the Murco Oil Depot with loaded tankers from Robeston, on 29 August 2009 is Class 60 No. 60 019 *Pathfinder Tours 30 Years of Rail Touring 1973-2003* (ex-*Wild Boar Fell*; later *Port of Grimsby and Immingham*) of DBS in EWS livery.

Stabled at Murco's Westerleigh Oil Depot on 23 January 2010 is Brush Class 60 No. 60 074 *Teenage Spirit* (ex-*Braeriach*) in DBS Teenage Cancer Prussian Blue livery.

Although it may not look it, this was the former Midland Railway's Leeds–Bristol main line – despite the weeds! Instead of proceeding along the former GWR main line from Westerleigh Junction to Temple Meads via Filton, Midland trains carried on via Fishponds to Temple Meads (or, until 1953, to St Philip's if a local). The Midland line now terminates at Murco's Westerleigh Oil Depot. Pictured is Brush Class 60 No. 60 009 (ex-*Carnedd Dafydd*) of DBS in EWS livery trundling through Westerleigh village on an oil tanker empties to Lindsey, 6 July 2010.

Brush Class 60 No. 60 071 *Ribblehead Viaduct* (ex-*Dorothy Garrod*) of DBS in EWS livery accelerates through Westerleigh village on a Westerleigh Oil Depot–Lindsey oil tank empties, August 2010.

In a rather misleading livery, DBS Brush Class 60 No. 60 084 (ex-*Cross Fell*) is in EWS-branded Trainload Freight livery – with no indication of its DBS ownership at all! It is seen at Yate on a Westerleigh Oil Depot–Lindsey oil tank empties, 1 September 2010.

Passing Yate at the same spot as the previous location is No. 60 096 (ex-*Ben Macdui*) of DBS but still in EWS livery on a Westerleigh–Lindsey oil tank empties, 30 September 2010. This and the similar tanker trains from Robeston have been long-standing duties of the Class 60s.

Looking resplendent in Tata Steel silver livery (or should that be steel livery?) Brush Class 60 No. 60 099 (ex-*Ben More Assynt*) of DBS is stabled at Westerleigh Oil Depot, 14 February 2011.

On the well-canted curve approaching Patchway, Brush Class 60 No. 60 100 (ex-*Boar of Badenoch*; later *Pride of Acton*) of DB Cargo in its bright red livery has its load well in hand on a Theale–Robeston empty bogie oil tanks train, 7 April 2017.

Chapter 13

BREL HSTs (Classes 41 and 43)

One of the star exhibits at the St Philip's Marsh 40th Anniversary of the HST Open Day on 2 May 2016 was the groundbreaking prototype HST – BREL (Crewe) Class 41 2,250 hp Bo-Bo No. 41 001 in BR Rail Grey and Rail Blue livery. After introduction the locomotive and coaches were reclassified as a DMU with the set numbered 252 001 and the former locomotive being designated power car No. 43000. After completing its passenger service it then saw departmental use as No. ADB 975812. It is very fortunate that this historic locomotive is preserved in working order as it presaged a revolution in intercity travel in Britain.

At the time classed as a DMU, HST set No. 253 019 in BR InterCity 125 Rail Blue and Grey livery does not have its set number on the front as it should have. At the rear of the set is power car No. W43038 (later Class 43 locomotive No. 43 038, then No. 43 238) and it is seen approaching Yatton on a Weston-super-Mare–Paddington service, October 1982. The locomotive was subsequently named *National Railway Museum The First Ten years 1975-1985*, then *City of Dundee* and lastly *National Railway Museum 40 Years 1975-2015*.

By May 1989, HST sets were classed as locomotives (Class 43) and trailers. Drawing into Temple Meads on a service from Paddington in May 1989 is No. 43 135 (later *Quaker Enterprise*) in BR InterCity Swallow livery. Although it should have its locomotive number on the side of the cab, it doesn't. I think this livery suited the HSTs best of all the many liveries they have carried over the decades.

Speeding past Chelvey near Nailsea & Backwell on a South West–North East cross-country service in June 1994 is Class 43 No. 43 089 (later *Rio Thunderer*, then *Hayabusa*). The set is in BR InterCity Swallow livery with the locomotive number on the cab side.

Still in original condition with a Valenta engine and covered marker light clusters, Class 43 No. 43 031 in First Great Western 'swish' livery has just arrived at Temple Meads on a service from Paddington, 13 July 2006. In my opinion the 'swish' livery is far more pleasing than the plain, unadorned FGW indigo-blue livery which succeeded it, thankfully now being replaced by GWR's retro Brunswick Green livery.

When Arriva Cross Country leased HSTs to relieve the hard-pressed and overloaded Voyagers, a variety of liveries appeared on the sets on cross-country services before Arriva's newly acquired sets could be repainted; thus much interest was added to the scene at Bristol. Seen under Temple Meads' impressive roof is a complete set in debranded Midland Main Line livery (with no indication of the operator) headed by Valenta-engined Class 43 No. 43 007 (later No. 43 207) on a Penzance–Dundee service, 23 May 2008.

Valenta-engined Class 43 No. 43 108 *St Andrews* (later No.43 308; formerly named *Old Course St Andrews*; *BBC Television Railwatch*) of National Express East Coast in their Interim blue livery on hire to Arriva Cross Country on a Manchester Piccadilly–Newquay 'Surfers Special' arriving at Bristol (Temple Meads), 24 May 2008.

Refurbished with a MTU engine and revised double-light clusters, Class 43/2 No. 43 309 (ex-No. 43 109; previously named *Scone Palace*; *Yorkshire Evening Press*) of National Express East Coast in their full livery heads coaches in NXEC's interim blue livery. The set is on hire to Arriva Cross Country and is seen on a Manchester Piccadilly–Newquay 'Surfers Special' at Temple Meads, 24 May 2008.

Emerging into the sunlight from a deep cutting at Newton St Loe to the west of Bath is First Great Western's Class 43/0 No. 43 029 on a Bristol Temple Meads–Paddington service, 8 February 2011. FGW refurbished its Class 43s in a similar way to National Express East Coast with MTU engines and separate twin light clusters.

At speed between Yatton and Nailsea & Backwell, Class 43/0 No. 43 042 of First Great Western is on a Weston-super-Mare–Paddington express, 23 April 2011.

FGW Class 43/0 No. 43 031 cruises past a field of maize at Newton St Loe on a Bristol Temple Meads–Paddington service, 31 July 2011.

Passing Barton Hill, with Bristol Temple Meads beyond, FGW Class 43/0 No. 43 134 (ex-*County of Somerset*) is on a Paddington–Weston-super-Mare service, 22 July 2012.

When Cross Country refurbished their Class 43s they too chose the MTU engine and the Class 43/2 nomenclature. Approaching at speed a public footpath crossing between Nailsea & Backwell and Yatton is Class 43/2 No. 43 357 (ex-No. 43 157 *HMS Penzance*, originally *Yorkshire Evening Post*) in Cross Country's distinctive livery on a Plymouth-bound service, 18 April 2014.

Cross Country's refurbished, MTU-engined Class 43/2 No. 43 321 (ex-No. 43 121 *West Yorkshire Metropolitan County*) speeds towards Wickwar Tunnel, north of Yate, on a Plymouth–Glasgow Central service, 18 April 2014.

Class 43/0 No. 43 194 (ex-*Royal Signals*) in First Great Western's indigo-blue livery approaches Keynsham on a Bristol Temple Meads–Paddington service, 10 June 2015.

On the embankment to the west of Keynsham, FGW's Class 43/0 No. 43 122 (ex-*South Yorkshire Metropolitan County*) is seen on a Bristol Temple Meads–Paddington service, 10 June 2015.

It is amazing to see the scale of vinyls that can now be applied to trains. On FGW's Class 43/0 No. 43 192 (ex-*City of Truro*) vinyls promoting Bristol 2015 European Green Capital have been applied, creating a very colourful impression. It has just arrived at Temple Meads on a service from Paddington on 17 March 2016.

An uncommon Class 43/2 on display at the St Philip's Marsh 40th Anniversary of the HST Open Day on 2 May 2016 was buffer-equipped No. 43 013 (formerly *Cross Country Voyager*, originally *University of Bristol*) of Network Rail in their yellow livery with additional Improving Your Railway branding. Network Rail refurbished their Class 43s with MTU engines and reclassified them 43/2. The buffer-equipped Class 43s were a group modified to act as 'surrogate DVTs' for temporary service on the newly electrified East Coast Main Line because the Class 91 locomotives were ready for service in 1989 before the Mk 4 coaches and DVTs had been completed. As an interim measure, sets of Mk 3 coaches were hauled/pushed by a Class 91 with a buffer-equipped Class 43 at the other end acting as an unpowered DVT – although after a while the diesel engine was put to work to provide additional power for the set.

Virgin Trains East Coast's Class 43/2s are not usually seen in Bristol! However, at the St Philip's Marsh 40th Anniversary of the HST Open Day on 2 May 2016 was No. 43 300 (ex-No. 43 100) *Craigentinny* (formerly *Blackpool Rock*) with additional '100 Craigentinny 1914–2014' branding. When GNER and its successor decided to refurbish their HST fleet they, like FGW, chose to replace the Paxman Valenta engines with MTU ones but for some reason reclassified the locomotives 43/2 rather than 43/0.

Paxman VP185-engined Class 43/0 No. 43 048 *TCB Miller* of East Midlands Trains in Stagecoach livery was also on display at the St Philip's Marsh HST 40th Anniversary HST Open Day on 2 June 2016. EMT was the successor franchisee to Midland Main Line, which had refurbished its HSTs; they, unlike other operators, did not pick MTU engines as replacements for the original Paxman Valentas but instead remained with Paxman, choosing their new 2,100 hp VP185 engine. The locomotives also received new light clusters although they retained three lights rather than going down to two, as other operators did. Curiously, although differently engined to FGW's MTU-engined Class 43/0s, MML chose the same nomenclature!

With First Great Western rebranding themselves as Great Western Railway, the livery was changed from indigo-blue to retro Brunswick Green. One of the first Class 43/0s to be so reliveried and rebranded was No. 43 187, which is seen at the St Philip's Marsh HST 40th Anniversary Open Day, 2 May 2016.

The rear gangway of a Class 43 is rarely seen clearly. At the St Philip's Marsh 40th Anniversary of the HST Open Day on 2 May 2016 is Grand Central's No. 43 423 (ex-No. 43 123) *Valenta 1972–2010*. Grand Central also chose the MTU engine when refurbishing their Class 43s, which they reclassified 43/2, as had GNER/NXEC.

There was a surprise unveiling at the St Philip's Marsh HST 40th Anniversary Open Day on 2 May 2016 when GWR's Class 43/0 No. W43002 *Sir Kenneth Grange* was newly named after the head of the design team for the HST. It was freshly repainted in the original BR 'Inter-City 125' HST livery and renumbered in the carriage series as simply a power car within a DMU set. No.W43002 had formerly been named *Techni?uest*, and originally *Top of the Pops*.

With some sunlight highlighting the power car in the late autumn gloom of Old Sodbury cutting, a South Wales–Paddington HST service nears Chipping Sodbury Tunnel on 29 November 2016. The train is headed by GWR Class 43/0 No. W43002 *Sir Kenneth Grange* (formerly *Techni?uest*, originally *Top of the Pops*) in the original BR 'Inter-City 125' livery.

Class 43/0 No. 43 165 *Prince Michael of Kent* (ex-*City of Edinburgh*) of GWR, but still in FGW's indigo-blue livery, surmounts Pilning Bank and nears Patchway station on a Swansea–Paddington service, 6 April 2017.

Sweeping through Patchway station is Class 43/0 No. 43 063 (previously *Rio Challenger*, *Maiden Voyager*) of GWR on a Cardiff Central–Paddington service, 6 April 2017.

Leaving Patchway station is Class 43/0 No. 43 026 *Michael Eavis* (ex-*City of Westminster*) on a Cardiff Central–Paddington service, 6 April 2017.

With newly erected electrification masts in the background, Class 43/0 No. 43 177 (ex-*University of Exeter*) of GWR enters the impressively deep Pilning Cutting as it approaches the Severn Tunnel on a Paddington–Swansea service, 6 April 2017.

Climbing out of the Severn Tunnel and tackling Pilning Bank on a Swansea–Paddington service on 6 April 2017 is No. 43 164 of GWR in FGW's indigo-blue livery, although the coaches and trailing Class 43/0 are in GWR's Brunswick Green livery.

Leaving Bath Spa on a Bristol Temple Meads–Paddington service on 6 April 2017 is Class 43/0 No. 43 180 (ex-*Rio Glory*; *City of Newcastle upon Tyne*) of GWR in FGW livery.

Class 43/0 No. 43 145 of GWR in FGW livery passes Weston Milton on the 13.00 Weston-super-Mare–Paddington service on 12 February 2018.

One of the exhibits at the HST 40th Anniversary event at St Philip's Marsh in May 2016 had been FGW's Class 43/0 No. 43 172 *Harry Patch – the last survivor of the trenches*. Here it is seen on 10 May 2018 at Bath Spa on a Bristol Temple Meads–Paddington service.

Chapter 14

GM (EMD) Class 59

When the WR's Class 52 'Western' diesel-hydraulics were being withdrawn in the 1970s, Foster Yeoman wanted to buy several for their own use on their Mendip Quarry stone trains because of the Class 52's high tractive effort and torque. At the time, objections from the rail unions scuppered the plans but by the 1980s times had changed. Yeoman were getting increasingly dissatisfied with the reliability of BR's Class 56s on their trains. In contrast, Yeoman were very pleased with the performance and reliability of their own shunters, which were products of General Motors (Electro Motive Division). Consequently, Yeoman ordered a small batch of GM's standard SD40-2 design but adapted for the British loading gauge as the Class 59. The locomotives proved extremely reliable with the result that orders from Amey Roadstone Construction (ARC) and National Power followed. Moreover, the Class 59s formed the basis for the later Class 66s, which became ubiquitous on Britain's railways. Seen here accelerating through Lawrence Hill on the Cranmore–Chester 'Chester Explorer' in September 2008 is GM (EMD) Class 59/0 No. 59 005 *Kenneth J Painter* in ARC livery, with Class 59/1 No. 59 104 *Village of Great Elm* in Hanson livery behind.

GM Class 59/2 3,300 hp Co-Co No. 59 206 *John F Yeoman, Rail Pioneer* (ex-*Pride of Ferrybridge*; *Vale of Belvoir*) of DBS in their red livery approaches Abbey Wood on a Network Rail ballast train, 22 April 2011.

Pictured near Yatton, GM Class 59/2 No. 59 205 *L. Keith McNair* (ex-*Vale of Evesham*) of DBS in EWS livery on a ballast train, 23 April 2011.

GM Class 59/1 No. 59 103 *Village of Mells* of Hanson is approaching Keynsham on 10 June 2015 on the 6A83 13.26 Avonmouth–West Drayton loaded bogie hoppers.

Chapter 15

GM (EMD) Class 66

When Wisconsin Central bought most of British Rail's freight operations on privatisation, they inherited a huge fleet of diesels which had an average age of over thirty years and were very unreliable by American standards. Even the well-regarded Class 47s were achieving only 65 per cent availability and required frequent overhauls. As a result, Wisconsin Central bought what they knew best – a GM (EMD) product. The JT42CWR design had a guaranteed availability rate of 95 per cent with minimum maintenance requirements. It was produced in large numbers as the Class 66 for English, Welsh & Scottish Railways, the name Wisconsin Central chose for their new UK operations. Freightliner, GB Railfreight and DRS followed EWS's example and ordered such numbers that the Class 66s are now Britain's most numerous locomotive class by far. Today coal traffic is fast disappearing but at a time when such trains were still common, GM Class 66/5 3,200 hp Co-Co No. 66 527 *Don Raider* of Freightliner is on a Didcot Power Station–Portbury empty coal hoppers train, held by signals at Temple Meads, 1 July 2008. Didcot power station is now long closed.

GM built a low-emissions version of the JT42CWR and approaching Yatton with an enormously long track relaying train on 16 August 2009 is Class 66/6 (LE) No. 66 623 *Bill Bolsover* (what a lovely name) in Bardon Aggregates livery.

A footbridge at Ram Hill, Coalpit Heath, used to offer a good vantage point for photographing trains but unfortunately the erection of security fencing has now negated good views. Here, Class 66/0 No. 66 553 of Freightliner is about to pass under the bridge on a Fiddlers' Ferry–Stoke Gifford Yard coal empties, 29 August 2009.

Freightliner's Class 66/9 Low Emissions Demonstrator No. 66 951 is pictured on the Calvert–Barrow Road RTS 'Binliner' at Easton Road Junction, Lawrence Hill, on 23 March 2011. The locomotive is about to back its train and switch tracks from the ex-GWR main line onto the link between the ex-GWR main line and what was once the Midland line (on the bridge in the background) to Temple Meads and St Philip's stations but which now terminates at the refuse transfer depot at Barrow Road. That was built on the site of the former St Philip's Goods Yard.

GM Class 66/5 No. 66 561 of Freightliner nears Parson Street on the Bristol–Tilbury 'Wineliner', 6 May 2011.

The very heavy Robeston/Lindsey–Westerleigh Oil Depot tanker trains have long been hauled by Brush Class 60s. However EWS, with their vast fleet of American-built Class 66s, decided to place their Class 60s into storage as non-standard, even though they had 100 of them! EWS's successor DB Schenker continued the same policy such that by early 2010 DBS were down to just a handful of active members of the Class 60 'fleet', used primarily for hauling the tanker trains to Murco's Westerleigh Oil Depot. DBS wished to withdraw these few Class 60s and trialled double-heading the oil trains with two Class 66s as one Class 66 could not match the tremendous torque of a Class 60. However, in the event double-heading was uneconomical and the oil trains reverted to Class 60 haulage very quickly. Surprisingly, this was followed by DBS taking many Class 60s out of storage and refurbishing them; the qualities of the Class 60s had finally been appreciated. The illustration shows Class 66/0s Nos 66 017 and 66 007 of DBS, still in EWS livery, reversing into Westerleigh Oil Depot with an oil tanker train from Robeston, 6 March 2010.

Low Emissions Class 66/7 No. 66 757 *West Somerset Railway* of GBRf looks resplendent at the St Philip's Marsh HST 40th Anniversary Open Day, 2 May 2016.

Seen in the deep Pilning Cutting and heading towards the Severn Tunnel is Class 66/0 No. 66 066 *Geoff Spencer* of DB Cargo, as DB Schenker was renamed, in its red livery on the 12.33 4B38 Acton Yard–Moreton-on-Lugg empty bogie hoppers, 4 April 2017.

Chapter 16

Alstom Class 67

Intended to replace Brush Class 47s on Royal Mail postal trains, the Alstom Class 67 3,200 hp Bo-Bos were a sophisticated, high-speed design that greatly improved postal services. However, only three years after their entry into service, EWS and Royal Mail failed to agree terms when negotiating the renewal of the mail contract. As a result, the Class 67s have been rather underused but expensive assets for most of their life. One passenger use they did find was serving festival goers to the Glastonbury music festival; First Great Western hired in stock for extra services from Bristol to Castle Cary, the nearest station to 'Glasto'. Stabled in the centre road in Temple Meads is EWS's Class 67 No.67 022 with a rake of debranded Virgin Mk 2f coaches hired to FGW for a 'Glastonbury Festival Special' on 30 June 2008. No. 67 026 was later to be named *Diamond Jubilee*.

A more regular – but relatively short-lived – passenger service that the Alstom Class 67 was used on was the Cardiff–Taunton service, which they took over from Class 57s. As with the Class 57s, the Class 67s topped-and-tailed this service, a seemingly wasteful practice for such expensive, powerful locomotives, but presumably suitable DVTs were unavailable. Departing Temple Meads for Cardiff Central is DBS's No. 67 017 *Arrow* in EWS livery on 25 March 2009.

Another duty on which Class 67s found themselves was the Summer Saturdays Bristol–Weymouth service. On such a service, No. 67 025 *Western Star* of DBS in EWS livery awaits departure at Temple Meads, 1 August 2009.

DBS's Royal Claret-liveried Class 67 No. 67 005 *Queen's Messenger* fills in for a failed GWR steam engine, *King Edward I*, on the Bristol–Paignton 'Torbay Express' speeding across the Somerset Levels near Yatton, 16 August 2009. At least this was a train that half-stretched the capabilities of the Class 67!

A second DBS Class 67 in Royal Claret livery is No. 67 006 *Royal Sovereign*. She is seen here gliding through Lawrence Hill on the Ealing Broadway–Gloucester 'Thames Tornado', November 2009.

On 6 July 2010, DBS's Class 67 No. 67 016 draws away from Abbey Wood on a Cardiff Central–Taunton service with a rake of Rail Blue and Grey-liveried Mk 2 coaches on hire to FGW.

Approaching Filton Abbey Wood a Cardiff Central–Taunton service comprises No. 67 018 *Keith Heller* (ex-*Rapid*) of DBS in 'Canadian' red livery with four debranded Anglia Mk 2 coaches and another Class 67 dead in tow, on hire to FGW, 2 August 2010.

Cruising through Sydney Gardens, Bath, is Class 67 No. 67 020 hauling LNER Gresley Class A4 4-6-2 No. 4492 *Dominion of New Zealand* (actually No. 60019 *Bittern* in disguise!) on the 'Bath Spa Express' from Poole, 14 September 2011. No. 4472 had run out of coal due to the non-delivery of a load at Westbury and continued its journey behind No. 67 020.

Alstom Class 67 No. 67 029 *Royal Diamond* of DBS, in EWS 'Management' livery, on hire to FGW slows for its stop at Abbey Wood on a Cardiff Central–Taunton service, 6 July 2010.

Chapter 17

Vossloh Class 68 and GE Class 70

In 2012, when DRS wanted a mixed-traffic locomotive – a concept that had seemingly gone out of fashion in the UK – existing designs such as the GM Class 66 and the GE Class 70 were clearly unsuitable for this requirement. As a consequence, Vossloh (now Stadler) amended their standard 'Eurolight' design to what they dubbed the 'UK Light' locomotive. Whether it is because the design is low in calories, I hesitate to speculate. The resultant Class 68 3,750 hp Bo-Bo is represented here by DRS's Nos 68 030 and 68 018 *Vigilant*, the former in DRS plain blue livery and the latter in 'Compass' livery. They are nearing Bristol Parkway on the 11.58 6M63 Bridgwater–Crewe nuclear flasks on 5 June 2018.

In 2007 Freightliner wanted to procure more fuel-efficient freight locomotives than the Class 66s and chose General Electric as supplier. This was the first time GE locomotives had worked in the UK. Seen at Stoke Gifford Yard, an almost brand-new General Electric Class 70 'Power Haul' 3,820 hp Co-Co No. 70 004 basks in the winter sunlight, 30 January 2010. But even the good weather cannot disguise the rather odd looks of the Class 70. No.70 004 was subsequently to be named *The Coal Industry Society* – yet another inspiring name.

Colas Rail was impressed by Freightliner's Class 70s and also ordered a batch. In rather dull weather, GE Class 70/8 No. 70 812 accelerates away from Patchway Junction on the 12.20 6C36 Westbury Lafarge–Aberthaw Cement Works empty cement tanks, 5 June 2018.

Chapter 18

BR/English Electric Class 73

Preserved BR/English Electric Class 73/1 electro-diesel 1,600 hp/600 hp Bo-Bo No. 73 101 *The Royal Alex* (ex-Nos 73 100; 73 801; 73 100, 73 101; E6007; formerly named *Brighton Evening Argus*) in Pullman livery at Bitton on the Avon Valley Railway, 23 May 2009. No. 73 101 is a long way from the Southern 750V dc third rail system! The Class 73s were built long before the term 'bi-mode' was thought of.

Chapter 19

Heritage DMUs (Classes 101–122)

The largest number of non-BR-built first-generation DMUs were constructed by Metropolitan Cammell of Washwood Heath, Birmingham. Two Class 101 local passenger three-car DMUs, each consisting of Class 101/1, 171 and 101/2 cars, in Rail Blue and Grey livery approach Nailsea & Backwell on a Weston-super-Mare–Bristol Temple Meads–Cardiff Central service in August 1982. Classes 101, 102 and 111, classified according to their engine manufacturers, were very similar to Metro-Cammell's earlier 'lightweight' design, which for some reason never received a TOPS classification.

Cruising along the Somerset Levels near Chelvey is Metro-Cammell (Washwood Heath) Class 101 (originally built as a Class 102) local passenger three-car DMU set No. C820 on a Cardiff–Bristol Temple Meads–Weston-super-Mare service in August 1982. The Class 101s were the longest-lived of any multi-car first-generation DMU, the first being built in 1956 and the last not being withdrawn until 2003. No. C820 was originally built as a Class 102 with BUT (Leyland) L680 engines but was re-engined – as were all Class 102s – with BUT (AEC) A220s and reclassified to 101.

Preserved BR (Derby) Class 107 two-car (originally three-car) local passenger DMU Nos Sc52006 (Class 107/2 DMBS) and Sc52025 (Class 107/1 DMCL) in BR green livery with yellow warning panels is at Oldland Common on the Avon Valley Railway, 28 October 2017. These were a heavyweight version of the Class 108 'Derby Lightweight' DMU and had similar short frames.

The BR (Derby) Class 108 local passenger DMU design was built in two-, three- and four-car sets and were a more modern version of their earlier unclassified 'lightweight' design, employing a similar alloy construction apart from a steel cab, which became the standard for all subsequent Derby builds. Approaching Lawrence Hill on a Bristol Temple Meads–Taunton service in September 1985 is Class 108 three-car DMU Set No. B590 consisting of Class 108/1, 161 and 108/2 cars in Rail Blue and Grey livery with all-yellow front ends (including windscreen surrounds) and black bufferbeams.

BR (Derby) Class 108 two-car local passenger DMU Set No. B962 consisting of Class 142 and 108/2 cars approaches Lawrence Hill on a Bristol (Temple Meads)–Taunton service, September 1985. The set has been refurbished and is in Rail Blue and Grey livery with yellow front ends and black window surrounds and red bufferbeams.

Arriving at Temple Meads on a Cardiff (Central)–Taunton service in June 1989 is refurbished BR (Derby) Class 108 two-car DMU set No. B970 consisting of cars No. 54207 (Class 142) and No. 53622 (Class 108/2).

At Nailsea & Backwell on a Bristol (Temple Meads)–Weston-super-Mare service in June 1989 is BR (Derby) Class 108 two-car DMU set No. B965 consisting of cars No. 53616 (Class 108/2) and No. 54209 (Class 142) in Rail Blue and Grey livery with all-yellow front ends.

Refurbished BR (Derby) Class 108 two-car set No. S940 with blanked-out headcode panels is in Rail Blue and Grey livery, with yellow front ends and black window surrounds; also, it has red bufferbeams. The set is awaiting departure at Temple Meads, June 1992.

The standard suburban DMU was of BR (Derby) design, although produced in a variety of formations, engines and builders. The most numerous of the Derby designs was the three-car Class 116. Many were based in South Wales and dominated the Valley services but were less frequent visitors to Bristol. However, seen here at Temple Meads on October 1990 is a Cardiff Canton-based unit, set No. C392, consisting of Class 116/2 and 116/1 driving cars and a Class 172 trailer, in Rail Blue and Grey livery. Note the Welsh dragon symbol. An HST lies in the adjacent platform, awaiting its passengers before departing for Paddington.

Pressed Steel of Linwood, Scotland, was one of the companies that won orders to build copies of the BR (Derby) Class 116 three-car suburban DMU. Pressed Steel's design was the Class 117 three-car DMU. Pictured is set No. B430 (later No. T305, then No. 117 305) consisting of cars Nos W51368 (Class 117/2), W59520 (Class 176) and W51410 (Class 117/1). It is approaching Yatton on a Weston-super-Mare–Bristol Temple Meads service in October 1982.

Pressed Steel (Linwood) three-car suburban DMU Class 117 Set No. B430 was specially repainted in BR (WR) chocolate and cream livery (but, incongruously, with all-yellow front ends) for the GWR 150th Anniversary Celebrations in June 1985. It is at Temple Meads awaiting departure on a special for the Portishead branch. There are currently attempts to reintroduce a Metro-style passenger service on this branch to relieve the heavy road traffic congestion that occurs in peak times, although previous attempts to do so have failed.

Birmingham Railway Carriage & Wagon Co. of Smethwick were another company that built copies of the BR (Derby) Class 116s. BRC&W Co. Class 118 suburban three-car DMU set No. P472 (composed of Class 118/1, 174 and 118/2 cars) is with another (unidentified) set approaching Nailsea & Backwell on a Cardiff (Central)–Weston-super-Mare service in June 1977.

BR's Swindon works produced the standard three-car Class 120 cross-country DMU but did not have sufficient capacity to produce the numbers needed in the time required. Therefore a contract was given to the Gloucester Railway Carriage & Wagon Co. to produce additional sets. However, the GRC&W Co. suggested that deliveries would be speeded up if certain features – such as the cab – of the standard Derby DMU be incorporated into the design as they were already tooled up to produce the Class 122 railcar, which was of standard Derby suburban design. The resulting Class 119 was therefore an amalgam of Swindon and Derby features as combined by Gloucester! GRC&W Co. Class 119 cross-country three-car DMU set No. B571 is about to leave Nailsea & Backwell on a Cardiff Central–Weston-super-Mare service in August 1977.

It seems a little odd that when a single railcar design was needed for branch lines with low usage, a single-car version of the BR Derby high-density suburban DMU was chosen. Two companies were contracted to produce the railcars, one of which was Pressed Steel. In effect a Class 117/2 driving motor brake with a cab at both ends, the Class 121 railcars proved highly flexible and were often used to strengthen three-car suburban sets at peaks or to tow a Pressed Steel Class 149 unpowered car to form a two-car DMU. They were the longest lived of any first-generation DMUs, being built in 1960 and with the last not being withdrawn until 2017. Although just one car, in the 1970s the original car numbers were supplemented by set numbers! Here Rail Blue set No. B132, car No.W55032, takes a nap at Severn Beach, as yet undisturbed by passengers, before taking a gentle stroll to Temple Meads in August 1980.

The Gloucester RC&W Co. version of the railcar was the Class 122 – effectively a double-cab, single-class version of the Class 119 motor brake composite. Set No. 106, car No. 55006, in Rail Blue and Grey, departs Temple Meads at full throttle for Severn Beach in June 1992.

Chapter 20

Modern DMUs
(Classes 143–166)

Designed as a cheap and cheerful solution to the problem of providing a value-for-money train for the less busy branch lines, the Class 143s have fulfilled that requirement – apart from maybe the 'cheerful' part. They have proved long-lived and reliable despite these 'glorified buses' never being popular and they are only now being replaced. The Regional Railways livery was one of the most attractive BR liveries, in my opinion, and this is carried by Alexander/Barclay Class 143 'Pacer' two-car DMU No. 143 625, pausing at Nailsea & Backwell on a Temple Meads–Weston-super-Mare service in June 1994 – hardly a branch line service!

Alexander/Barclay Class 143 'Pacer' (somewhat of a misnomer) No. 143 618 of First Great Western in 'Visit Bristol' promotional livery approaching Stapleton Road on an Avonmouth–Temple Meads service, 24 May 2008. On the right is the bridge which once carried another two lines and which is now being replaced by a new bridge to cater for the redoubling of the line from Dr Days Bridge Junction to Filton Junction.

Passing Easton Junction, Lawrence Hill, on a Temple Meads–Severn Beach service in March 2011 is Alexander/Barclay Class 143 'Pacer' two-car DMU No. 143 618 in First Great Western 'local lines' livery.

The BREL (York) Class 150 'Sprinter' DMU design was one of the first second-generation DMUs for main-line stopping, suburban and local services. The cars were based on the Mk 3 coach. Leaving Yate on a Weymouth–Gloucester service on a snowy January 2010 is Class 150/2 two-car DMU No. 150 248 of FGW in 'local lines' livery.

The BREL (York) Class 150/2 differed from the Class 150/1 in having inter-unit gangways and, when refurbished, lower-density seating. Leaving Yate is two-car DMU No. 150 267 of Arriva Trains Wales on hire to FGW on a Westbury–Gloucester service, 6 March 2010. FGW were suffering from a shortage of DMU stock at this time.

Seen at Newton St Loe is Class 150/1 two-car DMU No. 150 128 on a Temple Meads–Weymouth service, 24 July 2011. It was one of the first FGW DMUs to be repainted in plain indigo-blue livery rather than the usual 'local lines' variety. This unit was one of eight ex-London Overground/Silverlink units transferred to First Great Western after being displaced by new Class 170s. Their high-density seating and lack of inter-unit gangways didn't suit them for some of the longer services of FGW – such as the Weymouth service.

Repainted in the retro Brunswick Green livery of the rebranded GWR, Class 150/2 two-car DMU No. 150 248 (with a sister unit) approaches Patchway on a Weymouth–Great Malvern service on 6 April 2017.

Brunswick Green Class 150/0 'Prototype Sprinter' three-car DMU No. 150 002 of GWR leaves Keynsham on a Cardiff Central–Portsmouth Harbour service, 3 May 2018. The two Prototype Sprinters had been based all their lives in the London/Thames Valley area so presumably they were transferred to Bristol because of electrification – or should I say partial electrification – of the former area. This still seems a little odd, however, when younger sister Class 150s were being replaced in Bristol by Class 166s from London at the same time.

The Leyland Class 153 'Super Sprinter' diesel railcars were formed by breaking up the Class 155 two-car DMUs and fitting a very cramped cab to one end of each car, the work having been undertaken by Hunslet-Barclay. I have always thought it was something of a misnomer to dub both classes 'Super Sprinters' when they were built from Leyland National bus parts! And while they were fitted with lower-density seating than the Class 150 'Sprinters' as built, I would not regard them as equal to the refurbished Class 150s with 2+2 seating. Pictured is Class 153 railcar No. 153 373 of FGW, but still in Wessex Trains' 'Heart of Wessex' promotional livery, at Temple Meads on 24 July 2007.

Leaving Temple Meads for Severn Beach in January 2008 is Class 153 railcar No. 153 377 of FGW but still in the former franchisee Wessex Trains' attractive 'Scenic Lines of Devon & Cornwall' promotional livery.

At a time before most of the Class 155s were split into Class 153 railcars, Leyland Class 155 'Super Sprinter' two-car EMU No. 155 303 in BR Regional Railways livery with Sprinter logos awaits departure at Temple Meads on a Cardiff Central–Weston-super-Mare service, May 1989.

Another 'Super Sprinter' design intended for longer distance services than those operated by the 'Sprinters' was the Metro-Cammell Class 156 two-car DMU. Based on the Mk 3 coach, these live up to their name far more than the Class 155s do, to my mind. No. 156 438 in BR Regional Railways livery with Sprinter logos departs Temple Meads on a Taunton–Cardiff (Central) service, May 1989.

The BREL (Derby) 'Sprinter Express' completed the quartet of new-generation DMU types that BR procured to replace the first-generation DMUs of the 1950s and 1960s, the others being the Pacer, Sprinter and Super Sprinter. The Sprinter Express DMUs, based on the Mk 3 coach, were intended to replace many loco-hauled trains as well as DMUs on longer distance main-line and cross-country services. The most numerous 'Sprinter Express' units were the Class 158s. I have always thought highly of the Class 158s (and similar 159s) as they are easily the most comfortable and quiet of BR's second-generation DMUs – as, indeed, they were intended to be. But I also think they are more pleasurable to travel on than many more modern DMUs. At Bristol Temple Meads on a Brighton service in June 1992 is Class 158/0 two-car DMU No. 158 868 in the variety of BR Regional Railways livery that was specific to the Class 158s and with 'Regional Railways' branding as initially applied.

Alphaline was originally a BR brand of the 1990s specifically to be attached to some Class 158s with upgraded passenger facilities for the better provincial services that linked in with InterCity services. The brand was so popular that it continued under privatisation well into the 2000s. One company that stuck with the brand was Wales & Borders. Seen passing Bedminster on a Cardiff Central–Taunton service in April 2003 is Class 158/0 two-car DMU No. 158 817 branded Alphaline Wales & Borders in their attractive silver livery.

A pair of Class 158/0 two-car DMUs of FGW descend Horfield Bank at St Werburgh's on a Cardiff Central–Portsmouth Harbour service on 30 January 2008. One set is in debranded Wessex Trains Alphaline livery (No. 158 749) and one is in First Trans Pennine Express livery. Wessex Trains repainted the doors on its Alphaline silver Class 158s maroon to distinguish them from the Wales & Borders Alphaline units, which had blue doors. The train has just passed the bridge abutments which once carried the Midland 'Clifton Curve' line from the Midland Main Line to the Temple Meads–Clifton–Avonmouth branch.

Class 158/0 'Sprinter Express' two-car DMU No. 158 776 of FGW, but still in First Trans Pennine livery, approaches Abbey Wood on a Worcester–Weymouth service, 24 May 2008. The First Trans Pennine livery was a hybrid, having a First indigo-blue vinyl band on the lower body overlaid on Northern Spirit Trans Pennine maroon with a gold 'N', half of which was hidden by the blue band.

Arriving at Bristol Temple Meads on a service from Weymouth in August 2008 is a BREL (Derby) Class 158/0 'Sprinter Express' two-car DMU carrying a mix of liveries and branding. No. 158 750 of First Great Western has a First Group Indigo blue broad stripe on a base of BR Regional Railways Express livery with First Trans Pennine and First branding. The Royal Mail parcels conveyor bridge is hardly noticeable in the background.

Class 158s are unusual on the Severn Beach line but here we see GWR's No. 158 958 approaching Clifton Down station on the 15.15 Avonmouth–Bristol Temple Meads service, 23 May 2018. The 158/0 is still in the old First Great Western 'local lines' livery.

The Class 159s were built as BR Regional Railways Class 158s but converted to the specification of Network SouthEast for Waterloo–Exeter services, replacing coaches hauled by Class 50s, which were unsuited to the frequent stops of the service and becoming increasingly unreliable. They were initially branded as 'South Western Turbos'. Class 159/0 three-car DMU No. 159 104 (formerly named *City of Exeter*) of South West Trains in 'SWT Express' livery has left Bath on a Waterloo–Bristol Temple Meads service and is passing Newton St Loe, 19 March 2011.

Prior to privatisation, BR embarked on a programme of further DMU construction and one design was the Class 166 'Network Express Turbo' three-car DMUs built by ABB (York) for outer suburban services from Paddington to Oxford and Newbury. When these lines were electrified, the Class 166s were displaced by Class 387 'Electrostars' and transferred to the Bristol area. Pictured is No. 166 204 of GWR in their Brunswick Green livery on a Severn Beach–Avonmouth–Clifton–Bristol Temple Meads service at Redland, 10 August 2017. This service was the first in the Bristol area that the Class 166s worked.

GWR's Class 166/2 Network Express Turbo three-car DMU No. 166 206 nears Patchway Tunnel, South Wales bound, on 5 June 2018.

Chapter 21

Modern High-speed DMUs (Classes 220–221)

Following privatisation, Virgin chose to replace the HSTs and Class 47 loco-hauled cross-country trains with shorter 'Voyager' and 'Super Voyager' high-speed DMUs – although the potential to reach their 125 mph top speed on these services was limited. The cramped accommodation, noise and vibration compared poorly with the Mk 2 loco-hauled stock and especially the HSTs they replaced. Moreover, their short formations often resulted in overcrowding. And worse, Virgin's successor Arriva Cross Country took out the buffet to create more seating, which had only a marginal effect on overcrowding at the expense of a reasonable-quality catering service – a trolley service offering very limited fare and which might not get through the train because of the overcrowding is not an adequate substitute, in my opinion. Pictured is Bombardier (Wakefield & Brugge) Class 220 'Voyager' four-car DMU No. 220 016 (ex-*Clyde Voyager*) of Arriva Cross Country passing Bedminster on a York–Plymouth service in August 2009.

On a frosty morning on 17 January 2010, an unidentified Bombardier Class 220 'Voyager' four-car DMU of Arriva Cross Country crosses the viaduct taking the Great Western Main Line over the former Midland Birmingham–Bristol/Bath cross-country main line, which now terminates at the Murco oil depot at Westerleigh.

Bombardier Class 220 Voyager four-car DMU No. 220 008 (ex-*Ddraig Gymraig/Welsh Dragon*) of Arriva Cross Country on a Plymouth–Birmingham service is seen in Wickwar Cutting, 18 April 2014.

The Bombardier (Wakefield & Brugge) Class 221 'Super Voyagers' are similar to the 'Voyagers' but are of five-car formations and have tilting mechanisms on their bogies to allow higher speed around curves, although these are now locked out-of-use on the cross-country sets. Thus the narrow coach profile to allow the tilt and which partly resulted in the cramped accommodation has proved unnecessary. On a day when there was a light dusting of snow, speeding through Yate is Class 221 'Super Voyager' five-car DMU No. 221 121 (ex-*Charles Darwin*) of Arriva Cross Country on a Plymouth–Newcastle service, 9 January 2010.

Bombardier Class 221 'Super Voyager' five-car DMU No. 221 135 (ex-*Donald Campbell*) of Arriva Cross Country is seen at speed between Yatton and Nailsea & Backwell on a Plymouth–Birmingham New Street service, 23 May 2014.

Chapter 22

Hitachi IEP EMUs (Class 800)

The much-loved HSTs are now in the process of being replaced by Hitachi (Kasado & Newton Aycliffe) IEP – Intercity Express Programme – Class 800 bi-mode MUs. These are capable of operating in electric mode (25kV ac overhead) and with diesel engines over unelectrified tracks following the debacle of the late cancellation of parts of the electrification programme. Illustrated is Class 800/0 five-car BMU No. 800 012 of GWR sweeping through Patchway on a Newport–Paddington test train on 8 November 2017. Will the Class 800s ever be as popular as the HSTs?

GWR's Class 800/0 five-car BMU No. 800 006 in Brunswick Green livery leaves Bath Spa on the 12.00 Bristol (Temple Meads)–Paddington service, 29 December 2017.

Hitachi Class 800/0 No. 800 035 and a sister unit of GWR nearing Patchway Tunnel on the 11.45 Paddington–Swansea service, 5 June 2018.

Abbreviations

BMU	bi-mode multiple unit (electric MU with diesel engines for unelectrified lines)
BR	British Railways (1948–65), British Rail (1965–94/97)
BTC	British Transport Commission (1948–63)
BRC&W	Birmingham Railway Carriage & Wagon Co.
BREL	British Rail Engineering Ltd
DBC	Deutsche Bahn Cargo
DBS	Deutsche Bahn Schenker
DEMU	diesel electric multiple unit
DMU	diesel multiple unit (mechanical or hydraulic transmission)
ECS	empty coaching stock
ETH	electric train heating
EWS	English, Welsh & Scottish Railways
FGW	First Great Western
GBRf	GB Railfreight
GM (EMD)	General Motors (Electro Motive Division)
GRC&W	Gloucester Railway Carriage & Wagon Co.
GWR	Great Western Railway
HST	High Speed Train
MU	multiple unit
NSE	Network SouthEast sector of BR
SWT	South West Trains
TOPS	Total Operations Processing System
TMD	Traction Maintenance Depot
WR	Western Region of BR

Bibliography

Boocock, Colin, *Railway Liveries: BR Traction 1948–95* (Shepperton, Ian Allan Publishing Ltd, 2000).

Boocock, Colin, *Railway Liveries: Privatisation 1995–2000* (Shepperton, Ian Allan Publishing Ltd, 2001).

Cable, David, *Lost Liveries of Privatisation in Colour* (Hersham, Ian Allan Publishing, 2009).

Cable, David, *BR Passenger Sectors in Colour* (Hersham, Ian Allan Publishing, 2012).

Mackay, Stuart, *First Generation DMUs in Colour* (Shepperton, Ian Allan Publishing, 2006).

Maggs, Colin G., *Rail Centre: Bristol* (Shepperton, Ian Allan Publishing, 1996).

Marsden, Colin J., various parts of *Modern Locomotives Illustrated* (Stamford, Key Publishing Ltd, 2008 to date).

Marsden, Colin J., *HST Silver Jubilee* (Hersham, Ian Allan Publishing Ltd, 2001).

Marsden, Colin J., *HST The Second Millennium* (Hersham, Ian Allan Publishing Ltd, 2010).

Mitchell, Vic, and Keith Smith, *Country Railway Routes: Bath Green Park to Bristol* (Midhurst, Middleton Press, 1999).

Oakley, Mike, *Bristol Railway Stations 1840–2005* (Bristol, Redcliffe Press Ltd, 2006).